Adorning Your Crown:
Jewels for Everyday Living

By: Dr. Ashley D. Anderson

D1059921

ISBN: 9798410409605 (Paperback)
ISBN: 9798412327334 (Hardcover)

Front cover image by Ryan Kendall.
Book cover and interior design by Trevis Smith.
Edited by LaToya Turner, Creative Culture Editorial

Printed by Amazon Publishing, in the United States of America.

First printing edition 2022.

Dr. Ashley Anderson
PO Box 22923
Louisville, KY 40252

www.AshleyDAnderson.com

Dedication

To Atlas and Ace...my sons,

my inspiration,
my why...
Believe in the deepest parts of your heart that you
can do anything...you can.

Contents

Third Quarter:
Your Royal Preparation

Motivation
The Ultimate Virtue
The Wait
No Shame in a Setback
Are you willing to say I'm sorry?
Control your Emotions
Sparkle Face
Check your Position

Fourth Quarter:
Your Royal Mindset

Fight the Fear
Audacious Living
Just Do It
Free Your Mind
Stop and Think
Be Present
Ambition
Control
Insecurity
Quit Comparing
Vulnerability
Crown Yourself

Prologue
Reclaiming Your Crown

I've often heard that around the age of 40, we naturally begin to get comfortable in our own skin. We begin to own who we are and who we are not. We stop pretending and start living as the person we've always been without the pressure of trying to please the world. A woman I greatly admire, Judge Erica Lee Williams described this as "Level 3 Living." Well, I hit my Level 3 a couple years early. It took enduring the loss of my father, heartbreak, a failed marriage, and failed business partnership over the period of exactly one month to get me there early, but we are here.

This book, many years in the making is designed to be a 30-day guide to self-assessment and growth. It is my hope that regardless of your age, over the next 30 days, you can embrace who you are, decide who you want to be and begin the journey to get there, unapologetically.

I chose to be very candid in this book because I want each of you to know the truth. That life, no matter how beautiful it looks on social media, can hit you hard and the things that determine if/how you get to the other side are how you care for yourself, who's in your circle, and your mindset regarding the situation as well as the preparation it truly is for your future.

Regardless of where you are in your life right now, I want you to understand that you are royalty. Yes, I love some sparkle and a good shiny crown, but this is so much bigger than anything gaudy sitting on your head. Adorning your crown is about owning the essence of who you are. It's about taking the crown back that maybe you gave to someone else hoping that they'd put it on your head for you. It's about you designing your own crown. It's about putting it on your own head every single day no matter what. It's the symbolism of the crown that I want you to absorb. People who adorn their crowns daily desire more, require more, go after more. They embrace the greatness running through their veins and they set and enforce a higher standard for their lives. They wait for no one to see what's inside them before claiming their thrones. They just go for it. That's what I want you to do over this next 30 days. Wherever that crown is right now in your life, even if you have to construct a new one, grab it. Look in the mirror, wink one time, and crown yourself. You are worthy!

First Quarter:

Your Royal Self Care

because the world deserves the very best of you...

Who are you?

When Beyonce released her song/video "Formation," there were so many opinions about what she was saying or was not saying. Negative articles were written and shade was thrown, "... too black. ...not black enough. ...anti-police." In my opinion, "Formation" is a call to action; to be who you are unapologetically. Part of that is being accepting of your culture, your history, your appearance and not feeling the need to apologize to the world for it. This concept seems so simple yet so infrequently practiced. Beth Moore touches on this idea saying, "You cannot amputate your history from your destiny."

I often start my motivational speeches by asking the audience, "Who are you?" I start this way because I know that even the most fabulous and powerful words in all of the dictionary will be ineffective until you've come to terms with who you are and why you are where you are in life. I would absolutely NOT be the person I am today if it weren't for my days on 18th and Hill Street and 28th and Gaulbert. The ups, downs, triumphs, and failures have made me exactly who I am. This means I had to come to terms with my past, acknowledging ALL of it, learning and accepting the lessons in each situation I encountered, and then move forward.

In order to move forward we must be comfortable looking back. Growth is not about clinging to your past. It's about accepting it to determine why you are walking the path you are currently on. It's about using those things as evidence that you are more than a conqueror! Growth is all about becoming a victor and not allowing your past shortcomings to make you a victim.

When I ask who you are, I'm asking what makes you happy, what makes you sad, what calls you to action, what have you seen, heard or witnessed in life thus far that has brought you to where you are today? What are the nuances that make you unique? Through what lens do you see the world? What are your values? What are your boundaries? What are your deepest desires? What does love mean to you? What about peace? Happiness? What do you hope your legacy will look like?

Questions for Consideration

1. Reflect on the following, "Out of my greatest misery came my greatest strength." What strength of yours came from a dark place in your life?
2. Without using titles, labels, or things you do, answer the following question: Who are you?
3. What perception do others have of you? Is it consistent with your answer for question 2? Why or why not?

Jewel Challenge

Pause and deeply reflect over your life experience thus far. What have you overcome? How did you do it? Give yourself credit for the victories and get real with yourself about the shortcomings. Bottle those lessons and spend some time getting really clear about who you are. Use your past as a gift to inform your future purpose. Resist the urge to live a life you think is socially desirable and safe. Be authentically who you are and do what makes you happy. As they say...live your best life! Tell your story with strength and conviction, you just may save somebody!!

Reclaiming my Time

When Representative Maxine Waters repeated these words, "reclaiming my time," it went viral as it should have. Daily, we allow all sorts of things to monopolize our time and we need to purposefully reclaim it. Watching television, social media, playing video games, texting/talking on the phone, and living life without a plan are some habits we have that waste time everyday.

I spend a lot of time in my practice writing "homework lists" for my patients to encourage and remind them to do things like exercise, practice self-care, schedule alone time, or find a release for their stress. When I hear women say, "I don't have time," I ask what they can stop doing or what they can do less of in order to reach their personal goals. To me, those words translate to, "I'm not making time." Most often, we engage in things without thinking and we go from day to day without a real plan. We spend time saying things like, "I want to lose weight.. hate this job, one day I'll own my own business..These kids/this family/person drives me crazy and I need a break," and we never do it. If you can break down who wore what to the MET gala including descriptors of who made it and what it represents, you should be getting paid to write a fashion blog. If you have time to know the details of each Kardashian's love life and who did what on the Housewives shows, you have time to research that business idea.

To me, wasting time is worse than wasting money. You can always earn more money but time wasted is time lost...it's never coming back!

Every week, my cell phone gives me a screen time report. It tells me how much time I've spent on social networking, productivity apps, and entertainment, and how many times per day I pick up my phone and what apps I use most frequently. I realized with this report that I was spending six hours per week on Facebook and told myself that time could have been spent working on my book, I made that commitment in April, and by July, this book was complete. It was hard to create this new routine and there were days where I fell off but I held myself accountable to the deadlines I'd set. Sometimes I sacrificed a girls dinner or coffee date to get it done. Remember, there's a difference between being busy and being productive. We have to be intentional about how we spend our time. Each moment matters, how will you use it>

Questions for Consideration

1. Take an assessment of how you spend your time every day. What are 3 things you do that keep you "busy" but not productive?
2. About how much time each day are you spending on those activities?
3. Look at your list of goals. Write down ways you can better spend some or all of that time to be more productive toward your goals.

Jewel Challenge

Become the master of your time. Stop robbing yourself of your potential. It is true that we make time for what we want to — stop wishing, stop wasting and reclaim your time!

Taking Selah

Confession...I'm not a good rester. In fact, I'm writing this blog post at 4 a.m. It's after Ace's mid-morning mik request and the house is quiet. Usually, at this hour my mind has begun running through the checklist for the day. Usually, I find myself lying in bed mentally tossing around what things I could get done before the kids wake up if I just stay up and get to work.

There are also the days where I take the extra quiet time after my morning meditation to sit still with myself and take a Selah. In Hebrew prayer and song, the word Selah is often used at the end of a passage as a call to the reader to, "Stop and listen" before moving on. This word is used over 70 times in the Bible, mostly in the book of Psalms. Some commentators believe that Selah was a musical notation possibly meaning, "Silence" or "Pause," which is an opportunity to allow all that's been sung about prior to sink in — a moment to truly bask in the presence of the Lord.

I suggest that Selah is necessary beyond music. It's necessary in life. You can read all you want, recite all of the positive quotes, affirmations, and scriptures that your brain can memorize but until you absorb those things deep into your being, it's nothing but theory and lip service. There truly is no impact without the pause. I wonder sometimes how life can get so far away from us — how we can drift so far from our purpose, boundaries and value system. I believe it's because as a culture, we pride ourselves in staying busy, going from project to project, goal to goal, and achievement to achievement without the Selah.

Without the Selah, you cannot evaluate how you feel and whether or not you're truly happy. Without it, you cannot be clear about the path on which you should walk. You cannot truly even celebrate how far you've come and all you've overcome without the Selah. You see, Selah is the necessary pregnant pause. It is really the moment that allows you to go deep within yourself to ask questions and await the answer. "Is this job/career for me?" "Is this person the partner God created for me to fulfill my purpose alongside of?" "Am I happy?" "Do I have peace?" "Am I showing up every day in a way that best represents who I am and who I desire to become?" "Am I who I say I am?" "What lessons can I learn from this season of hardship, pain, or abundance?" Selah.

Questions for Consideration

1. Why do we so often find ourselves at the end of our own priority lists?
2. What are you actively doing to invest in yourself?
3. Think about your circle. Who holds you accountable to take care of yourself?

Jewel Challenge

Schedule time for yourself. Block out time to address your own needs, or even to just spend a few minutes alone with your own thoughts. Block at least one full day per month as a mental health day and do absolutely nothing on a schedule. Daily, create space to sit still and reflect. Allow yourself to assess things from the inside out. I read a quote once that said, " Now and then it's good to pause in our pursuit of happiness and just be happy." This couldn't be more true. We are human beings, not human doings. Take the time to stop doing and just, Selah.

Your Smile is Your Job

There's a patient of mine that I remember very vividly. She entered my office in tears one day stating she was certain something was wrong with her and that she needed medication for depression and anxiety. She had been married within the last year and had recently become a mother. Her career was right on track and she had a great support system. She was active in the community and well liked by her peers. Yet, she sat there in a puddle of tears confessing her unhappiness. As I listened to her intently, I heard what I hear from so many women; she was donning her next hat before she even got the first one off. When she finished talking, I asked her one question that ultimately opened the floodgates. I asked, "What are you doing for yourself?" After more tears and a few hugs, she confessed, "nothing." While she was busy investing time and energy into everyone around her, she was saving nothing for herself. Haven't we all been there? I know I have! I've been told repeatedly that you cannot pour from an empty cup but it seems so hard to prioritize yourself sometimes. Ultimately happiness starts with you — Not with your relationships, job, or friends.

This means that we have to do the work on ourselves. We must take care of ourselves and we must be accountable to ourselves, for ourselves. It's easy to stay busy being busy and never stop doing the things that make us happy, but it's our responsibility. When we don't do it and we feel bad, it's no one's fault but our own.

In "*When Mars and Venus Collide,*" John Gray states, "A woman's greatest challenge is to begin caring for herself as much as she is caring for others...when she takes the time to feel good herself, a woman can then allow her partner to bring her up to feeling great."I believe this applies to both men and women. It applies to intimate relationships, parenting, work life — just life in general. When we take care of ourselves,we can be happy, at peace, and ready when that great opportunity presents itself.

I suggest that we must strategically invest in our own happiness. There's no way around it and it's only a matter of time before you fall apart if you don't. I've been setting my alarm to wake up at 5am to have some alone time while the house is still silent. I use this time to read, pray, mediate, and just sit still. Regardless of the activity, it helps me to start my day off grounded and peaceful. I am also very big on routinely scheduling "girl time" where I can take off ALL hats and just be Ashley. It's imperative to my happiness and sanity which ultimately helps me to be a better woman, mother, and business owner. Maybe your "thing" is your gym time, a routine nail appointment, or a massage. Whatever it is, make sure you are doing what you need to make you feel like you are a person separate from all the things you do. In the words of my mentor and mommy Miss Denise, "you are a human BEING, not a human DOING!"

Questions for Consideration

1. Why do you think it's so hard to prioritize self-care?
2. Think through a full day in your life. What are you doing regularly for you? What about last week?
3. Take a moment to reflect on your mood/feelings in the last couple of days. Are you truly happy right now? Why/why not?

Jewel Challenge

Schedule some "you time" every day. Protect this time on your calendar just like it was any other meeting or appointment that you'd prioritize. Even if it's only 10 or 15 minutes per day to sit in a quiet room and meditate, find it. Schedule it. Protect it. Trust me, you will feel better!

Speak your Truth

Everyone always says that kids speak the truth and mine are no different. Especially as Atlas has started attending school and expanding his vocabulary, he's gotten a lot more vocal with his opinions and is teaching Ace to do the same. Recently, Atlas asked for pepperoni pizza wraps for his lunch. Y'all, I slaved over these wraps and even let him see the finished product as I placed them in his lunch box for the next day. I was so excited picking him up from school to hear how much he loved them. He got in the car, and before I could finish asking how his lunch was, he said, "mommy, I didn't like my lunch." I was crushed! But was also so proud of him for speaking his little mind. Most adults wouldn't have been that honest. Although my taste test proved the wraps to be wonderful, he did not think so and he was not afraid to say so.

I use this illustration to remind each of us that we were born to be unique. We were not placed here to be clones of others. I've been employed in places where diversity in opinion was not valued. I've been in friendships and relationships where my truth was not honored or had consequences that ultimately led to the demise of the relationship. It can be scary to speak your truth and stay true to your values. In fact, I'm convinced that the lack of transparency that exists so often in our relationships is what leads to resentment, unhappiness, infidelity, and the ever-so-common midlife crisis. Royalty, you were not designed to function like a volcano keeping things in until you explode. It is not healthy.

Remember that much of what we say or need to say can fall upon receptive ears if we are mindful of our delivery. If I approach my friend and I snap at him/her with head jerking and eyes rolling to tell them that something they've done has hurt my feelings or rubbed me the wrong way, I should expect them to react defensively with the same tone which ultimately will lead to an argument. Instead of allowing my fiery side to be in control, I make myself step away and think. *Is this something that if it happens again will upset me?* If the answer is yes, I will think about the best way to address the situation when I am calm and can clearly get my point across. It serves no one for me to stay quiet for the sake of keeping the peace.

We must stop getting ourselves into situations we know we don't want to be in because we don't want to tell the truth. That is no way to live. You must be willing to suffer a bit of discomfort in order to achieve the change or happiness you deserve in life. Iyanla Vanzant says, "Love people enough to tell them the truth, and respect them enough to know that they can handle it." This quote says so much. Being a truth teller in today's society may make you a rare commodity and it may be very uncomfortable. However, it makes you real and it makes you respectable. Do not shrink from the truth no matter what's going on around you. Share your truth but do so with love and respect. Even if others don't agree with your truth, they will respect the fact that you didn't lie or deceive them. Hey, it got Atlas a new recipe for lunch that he actually loved! Stop living in silence. Speak your truth.

Questions for Consideration

1. Do you routinely speak your truth? Why or why not?
2. Why do so many of us shy away from giving our honest opinions and telling those we say we care about how we truly feel?
3. Compare and contrast the long-term effects of speaking your truth versus NOT speaking your truth. Which life will you choose from this day forward?

Jewel Challenge

Speak your truth with eloquent thunder. Do not bite your tongue when you know you should interject. Allow your voice to be heard because you deserve that and your integrity depends upon it!

Embracing No

It is impossible to be everything to everybody and still have anything left to give the people that mean the most to you. In my adult life, I've had the hardest time with truly finding balance. I used to pride myself in being able to pursue all my goals and basically, to have it all. I've always wanted to be the wife, the mom, the philanthropist, and the successful business woman — just that super boss babe that could do it all. What I've realized though, is that sometimes, in order to have it all, you have to say no.

No — a two letter word, just one syllable, but goodness, it can be so hard to say. As women, we have the hardest time with this word. I wonder sometimes if it's our culture that engrains in us the idea that we have to be superwoman in order to be considered a great mother, a great partner, and to have a career, so that you're not seen by the world as weak, fragile, needing support, and having nothing of substance to offer. Let's be honest here for a second. Women, we haze each other far too much. We post our prettiest faces on social media portraying the image that we always have it together and that being a significant other, a parent, and a career woman is easy. We post as if there are no rough days and we should always be happy and eager to serve in any of these roles when it's time. In reality, this type of image perpetuation is exactly what leads women to my office in tears, filled with anxiety, asking for medications to help them do better, be better, and be happy in the life they've built and have always thought they wanted to have. The truth is, some days just plain suck and feeling overwhelmed or at your wits end, is very normal. Let's face it, sometimes we need to literally take our capes off to protect our sanity. Now, I'm not suggesting we push the needle all the way to the other side of the record, but it is time to be a bit more strategic.

What makes you happy? Are you spending the majority of your time doing the things that make your heart smile? There's no way that you can sustain spending your whole day working to please and serve other people and then spending your nights crying in the shower because you're unhappy or you don't have peace. Here's something we have to think about: What are we showing our daughters? What are we showing the young ladies that will come behind us, watching our every move and are wanting to walk in our footsteps? What are we teaching our sons/daughters that they will look for in their future partners? Simply put: It takes a superwoman to be able to say no and to realize that she has to prioritize the things that are most important to her in order to be truly successful. It's time to say no to all the extra things that you are doing just because you were asked.

Sometimes this even means saying no to family and that's one of the hardest things to do. For some reason the more we add to our plates or the more we get our own lives in order, the more we feel like we must take on the burdens of others. Sometimes those burdens are financial, emotional, or spiritual, and they are draining. It's like I said before, you can't be everything to everybody and have nothing left for the people and things you love. You can't answer the phone every time someone's in a crisis or just having a bad day and taking on their negative energy. You may think you're helping, but at the end of the day, what you're doing is taking energy and positivity from your family, business, and day in general. Now, this may come across as harsh, but the question you have to ask yourself is: *Are you willing to sacrifice your peace of mind for the sake of making someone else feel good in a situation that they've put themselves in?* It is about protecting your peace and it's about giving yourself what you deserve. Life is too short for you to walk around having guilt and feeling down in the dumps because someone else gave you their negative energy. Say no. You must guard what goes into your mind. You must guard the types of thoughts and feelings and energy that enter your circle and rub off on you; it does matter.

So...what is the litmus test for the big NO? I'm so glad you asked!

- If you know you really don't have time- NO
- If you're just trying to be nice- NO
- If it's going to compromise or complicate decisions and plans you've already made for your family- NO
- If you are not passionate about the cause- NO
- If you're already exhausted- NO

- If you already are not using the time you do have left to practice self-care- NO

You get the picture! It's time to be selective about the things and people we sign up for. Just say NO...it will protect your peace!

Questions for Consideration

1. Why do you think it is so hard to say no?
2. What are some things you have recently said YES to when you should have said NO?
3. What can you do to better value your time and your sanity, so that you can say NO the next time you need to?

Jewel Challenge

Trust your gut...you normally know when it's time to say no, decline that call, or take a moment for yourself. Honor that feeling. Be polite but be direct. "Thank you for asking, but I'm unable to commit to that at this time." Don't apologize, don't give an excuse, just plain, NO. Remember, your value is not determined by how much you sacrifice yourself to make others happy.

Set Your Boundaries

"One of the most courageous decisions you will ever make is to finally let go of what is hurting your heart and soul." ~Brigitte Nicole

As I've said before, learning to say we are sorry is one of the most important relationship skills you can ever develop, but what if you're the one who's been wronged? What if your heart has been hurt so badly that all you can do is crawl in the bed and cry? Have you been there? I have! How do you get past that hurt and pain? When someone, especially someone you care about, does something so wrong it shakes you to your core? Ultimately, you must get past it — not for the sake of that other person but for the sake of having peace in your own heart.

First, you must understand that when others are operating from a place of brokenness, pain, or hurt, they will have a hard time owning their wrongdoings or even saying they are sorry. It is said that when people know better, they do better. If all you know is constant conflict, dysfunction, angry outbursts, lying, and the retraction of love, that is your understanding and concept of normal. Because they are unable or unwilling to unpack their own past baggage, they may have moved on with life as if nothing at all has happened. They will often repeat the same cycle over and over in their lives, labeling themselves as the victim when the whole while, they are unable to recognize that they are the unchanging and consistent factor in each of the failed relationships. Likewise, if you are accustomed to speaking to others with love or to seek resolution to conflict, that will be your function in the relationship. Try not to take it personally. They may be unable to be what you need right now or you may need to teach them how to be in your life and how to handle conflict when you are involved.

In that instance, check your reaction. Instead of losing your cool and allowing their mess to ruin your day, take a deep breath and realize that right now, it may be best for you to love that person from a distance. When someone hurts you, it is your responsibility to speak up. We often lick our wounds and just wait and hope for the day to come that things get back to normal but you must set boundaries. When things cool down, address your offender, and let them know what they did to hurt you. Discuss ways this can be prevented in the future and make sure they understand the depth of the pain that was caused. Remember you're not doing this to reopen the wound but if you don't address the situation fully and truthfully, it will most likely happen again or you will live silently in misery and allow anger and resentment to eat away at you. Ladies, we are notorious for doing this in our intimate relationships and we have to stop. It is your job to teach people how to treat you. Build boundaries and make others respect them. If there is anyone not willing to do this, it is time for them to go. PERIOD.

Questions for Consideration

1. Why do you think we silently carry the hurt of past wrongs and hurts instead of addressing our offenders so that we can move on?
2. What hurt are you carrying that you need to address in order to set yourself free?
3. For those offenders who we can no longer address but who have scarred us, what do you need to do in order to let go of that hurt? Create a plan and work toward that.

Jewel Challenge

We can teach people how to treat us by enforcing the boundaries we set. This does not mean that people will always respect your boundaries. People will hurt your feelings, disrespect you, and sometimes do things that in your opinion are inconceivable. Don't hold grudges or allow bitterness to set up in your heart. Pivot. Readjust your boundaries so they can no longer hurt or disappoint you. There's no need to be mean or nasty in return. We don't need to get them back. We don't need to try to make them feel what we felt. Keep it moving. Life has a way of correcting all wrongs. That is not your job. Your job is to stay focused on your goals and live each day to the fullest. Let your offender suffer by watching your royal elevation from the front row. That, my brothers and sisters, is my challenge for you.

Second Quarter:
Your Royal Cadre

because energy is transferrable...

Who's in the arena with you?

A couple of months after I got married, I found myself in a very dark place. While still high on married life, I was dealing with loss internally. We'd discovered the week after the wedding that we were expecting, and suffered a miscarriage the next day. The rollercoaster of celebrating new life and mourning the loss in less than 24 hours was unexplainable. I felt guilty at that moment. I'd married the man of my dreams in a wedding more amazing than anything I could've fathomed. I didn't have room to complain about anything, so I didn't. I shed a few tears and then as always, I kept moving. I kept moving until month two of trying to conceive again. When my cycle came, I found myself sobbing in my office bathroom. I was devastated. That time, I was so sure I was pregnant. I'd had all the symptoms. In a matter of seconds, I badgered myself with a myriad of questions:

What was wrong with me?
Why weren't we getting pregnant?
Did I wait too long?
Was this a punishment for something I'd done wrong in the past?

As I stood there and stared into the mirror with tears and snot streaming down my face, I realized that I needed my tribe. Yes, I had a partner who said he would do absolutely anything to take away my pain but I also needed Djuan who empathized with me

36

and made me laugh. I needed Mo to tell me I was stressed and needed to find ways to relax my mind and body. I needed Jessica and Toya who told me they were praying for us, that this was a process, and God would not fail me. I needed Tab and Tawana who told me I wasn't crazy, they loved me, and they anticipated the call that their niece or nephew was on the way. I needed Justin who told me that I was the peanut butter to his jelly and he would support me in whatever way I needed. I needed Shonda who reminded me of my strength and that in time it would happen.

At that moment, when I couldn't see past my pain and disappointment, I knew I needed my tribe to hold me up. I needed their strength, their love, and their advice. I needed for them to be a sounding board that allowed me to vent and share the feelings I wasn't ready to share publicly.

In the last two years, I've experienced some of the hardest moments of my life. Publicly, things seemed fine, but I was falling apart inside. I had manage the loss of my father at the same time I was grieving the end of a marriage I thought was forever. I was grieving the exit of my business partner from a business we had planned to feed our families for generation, and only my inner circle knew. I once wrote that you never knew how strong your circle was until you needed them to hold you up. My circle did just that. In so many ways, (those listed here and more) held me up when I was in need. They were in the arena with me when the lights were off, when nobody was looking, and when things were ugly. They were always ready to go to war with and for me and that support went further than words could describe. Who is in the arena with you? Check your circle today. It can make you or break you.

Questions for Consideration

1. What situations/feelings are you holding on to that your circle can help you through?
2. Many people say, "I don't like telling ANYONE my personal business," but everybody needs at LEAST one person they can keep it real with. Who is your person (people)?
3. Typically, different people in your circle provide different types of support for you. In what way canmeach person support you?

Jewel Challenge

Reach out to your circle today and thank them for standing in the arena with you. Share something you're currently dealing with and could use some support working through. Ask if there is anything that you can do to support them.

Blocking Naysayers

I read a column in the newspaper entitled, "Parents Dismiss Teen's Aspirations." In short, the teen dreamed of becoming an astronaut but because her parents didn't think that career would be lucrative enough for the lifestyle they envisioned for her, they wanted her to become a doctor or lawyer instead. As far as they were concerned, those were her only two career options. As I read that article, my heart broke. I've been there. I've set significant goals for myself only to have people I loved and respected tell me I couldn't or shouldn't. I've succumbed to these naysayers more than I'd like to admit. I've passed up home/property ownership, business opportunities, opportunities for travel, and even reconsidered relationships because folks planted seeds of doubt. I almost didn't start Athena Health and Wellness because I repeatedly heard that I was crazy, I could never compete with the healthcare typhoons in town, or I should continue to work for someone else for the sake of financial security. Haven't we all experienced this?

What should that teenager have done? If she was someone you loved and cared about, would you have told her to be obedient and possibly live in regret or become defiant and risk losing the support of her parents? I hate to be the one that tells a teenager to block out their parents voice, but sometimes it must be done. This also goes for adults! Sometimes folks cannot see what you see, and that's OK. Understand that your vision may not always be understood or accepted by those around you, even those who are closest to you. Although they may love and support you, they can stifle your growth by speaking negatively and discouragingly toward your aspirations because they can't see your bigger picture nor do they know the calling that has been placed upon your life.

In high school, it was my dream to work as a professional model. It hurt me deeply for friends and family members to laugh and say it was stupid and would never happen. There was no way this little tomboy from the West End of Louisville could believe that she could or should make any type of splash in the beauty industry. I bottled that dream up and worked toward it in silence. I signed myself up for every legit modeling and self-improvement class that I could afford from my Showcase Cinemas paycheck. I practiced walking and posing in every free and alone moment I had. I studied the pages of fashion magazines when I could get my hands on them. I even started designing and sewing my own clothing.

A few years later, when I arrived home from a month of working as a model in China, those same people were saying, "That's my girl! I'm so proud." They couldn't see it, but because I knew it was something that I was supposed to do, I persisted. I put my blinders on and went for it. For this reason and others, it's sometimes best to keep your biggest dreams private. As Michelle Obama says, "Failure is a feeling long before it is an actual result." You cannot afford to allow the naysayers in your life — whether friend, family, or foe — to have the victory over your mindset. You just cannot allow it.

One of my other favorite quotes is from Bishop TD Jakes. He once said, "When you are a giraffe and receive criticism from turtles, they are reporting the view from the level they are on. To get to the core of who you are, you need to understand what you are." Stop allowing turtles to pull you down to their level. Stand tall in your purpose and walk toward that vision uninhibited and unapologetically. Your future depends on it!

Questions for Consideration

1. Describe a time you felt like a naysayer threatened a goal you had for yourself. How did it make you feel? How did you respond?

2. What is a goal you are actively working toward (or should be working toward) that you should keep off the radar until it comes to fruition?

3. Why do you think we feel the urge to share our goals and dreams and seek approval from others?

Jewel Challenge

Watch who and what you listen to. Trust your heart and follow your passion. Even if they don't necessarily agree, the people who love you will respect you for it. At the end of each day you have to look at yourself in the mirror. Make sure you're able to do that with a wink and a smile saying..."I'm proud you're going for it." That is a victory! The only failure is not trying at all. Commit yourself to working feverishly on your goals without broadcasting them to any turtles that may throw you off your game! That means keep them off of social media, y'all!

Who's Clapping?

In 2014, I ran for state representative. As I was being prepped for the campaign, I was given all sorts of advice and warnings of things to be prepared for. One of the things I will never forget was making "the list." I was asked to compile a list of everyone I knew that I could ask for support — to either volunteer or donate to the campaign. As I worked on that list, I was told repeatedly that I would be surprised at the people who showed up for me and also at those who did not. Just as they said, I was shocked...some of the people I just KNEW would be there were not and many I never even thought to ask, showed up. I can't lie to you,, it really hurt my feelings. I can't say I have showed up for every event for every friend, but I try my best. I'm thankful for this lesson though, because as life progressed, even fewer showed up for me. At every major life transition, I've lost people I deemed part of my circle because for whatever reason, they couldn't clap for me when it was my turn to win.

When I got engaged, I lost some friends; when I started a business, and got married, I lost more. During the loss of our first pregnancy and into my pregnancy with Atlas, I lost more. and even more with the second pregnancy. During marital trials and divorce, you guessed it, I lost more.

In life though, you realize that there are people who are there for you simply for photo ops but they are not truly there to celebrate with and for you. Although it may hurt or be disappointing, it's

OK to let it and let them go.

Understand that when others are operating from a place of brokenness, pain, or hurt, they will have a hard time clapping for you when you win. Try not to take it personal. It doesn't necessarily mean they don't love you and aren't happy for you, they just can't be what you need in that moment. Check your reaction. Instead of losing your cool and allowing their mess to ruin your day/moment/vibe, take a deep breath and realize that right now, it may be best for you to love that person from a distance. Your growth, success, and dream come true could be another person's nightmare. Pay attention to who claps when you win and who's there for the grind. While there is power in restraint and stillness, sometimes you need to let go. Friendships are two-sided — reciprocal and supportive. Instead of being upset when folks reveal themselves, count it a blessing. You don't want snakes in your garden!

Questions for Consideration

1. Think of a time when you were disappointed by the behavior of someone in your circle during one of your big moments. How did it make you feel?
2. How has your circle changed over the years as your life has evolved?
3. Are you actively supporting those in your circle the way you'd like them to support you? If your answer is no, do better today!

Jewel Challenge

Sometimes it hurts to let people go but you have to. Take back the power you have given others to upset your day. No one deserves that kind of power over you. Remember, the smallest hole can cause even the greatest ship to sink. Check your circle.

Third Quarter:

Your Royal Preparation

because we all need to be pruned...

Motivation

When I competed in pageants, I used to carry a photo of my brother during interviews and on-stage competitions. Sometimes I had it tucked away in a pocket and other times it was in my bra, but it was always there. During those years, he was my motivation to be successful. I'd spent his whole life telling him to dream big and that he could be anything he wanted to be in life, so I had to walk the walk to prove it. Even in some of my scariest moments, like walking on stage in China representing the USA in front of an audience of tens of thousands, he was there reminding me to push through and my reasons why. When I competed in fitness competitions later in life, the background on my cell phone was a photo of the lean body I was working toward. When I was working on my dissertation, even though I quit a million times in my head, the screensaver on my laptop was a motivational quote reminding me to see it through. No matter the journey I was on, I knew there would be tough times and during those moments, I needed to be sure I had positive reinforcement on deck.

Today, I have a vision board that is strategically placed in my bedroom on the way to the bathroom. That way, when I wake up in the morning, its one of the first things I see. On the wall directly in front of my bed is a quote that says, "Happy moments, praise God. Difficult moments, seek God. Quiet moments, worship God. Painful moments, trust God. Every moment, thank God."

The screensaver on my phone is a picture of my dream home with the words, "the universe is conspiring in your favor." No matter which way I look when I wake up, there's positive reinforcement and that is intentional.

What motivates you? In the dark moments, what reminds you of your why?

Sometimes, when life hits us and we become overwhelmed and exhausted, we lose motivation. In those moments, it seems easier to shut down and quit. Its in those moments that we need to have reminders strategically placed in our lives to keep us going. Remember, if you set yourself up for success, anything is possible!

Questions for Consideration

1. What is your why? Why are you pursuing the things you are in life?
2. Take a moment to think of a way to keep your "why" at the forefront of your mind. Where can you place it to keep you motivated consistently?
3. Reward yourself for the small victories. Remember that it is ok to celebrate yourself and allow yourself a break from your hard work.

Jewel Challenge

Find your why and celebrate your wins. Remember that your purpose is bigger than any one person or situation. You know yourself better than anyone. Plan for success today by planning to overcome the inevitable bad days. Set yourself up to WIN!

The Ultimate Virtue

Everyone says patience is a virtue. It's something we grow up hearing "grown folks" tell us when we aren't getting what we want, when we want it. "Calm down." "Be patient." "Your time will come." "Why are you in such a hurry?"

As a Type A personality, I must confess that I am very goal/action oriented. I'm a Sagittarius and can be impulsive, so when I want something, I want it NOW! Throughout my career, if I set a goal, I wanted to pursue it immediately. I wanted to become a nurse practitioner, so I applied to the Master's program, was accepted, and started that same summer. I wanted to start a women's health practice, so I began meeting weekly with my former business partner and we got it done in eight months. I don't believe in wasting time. While this method has been greatly successful at times during my career, it hasn't been so successful in other, more personal matters.

When we hurry in life, we rush things that shouldn't be rushed — relationships, marriages, having children with the wrong people, relocating to the wrong city, accepting the wrong job, etc. One thing I've learned the hard way is that God often gives us one of three answers when we ask for something: yes, *no, and not now.* The yes and no, I can normally handle but the *"not now"* drives me insane. *Ok, not now, but when? I'm ready. Can't you see that?*

For months, I spent my mornings in tears on the floor of the guest bathroom, pleading to God to save my marriage. I'd done prayer challenges, fasted, and a 40 day love dare. I sought advice and prayer from the seasoned saints in my life as well as my Pastor. I was sure that God would bless the covering I'd prayed over our home and my commitment to honor the promise I'd made to him just 4 years before. But He said no, and every time I tried again, His "no" got louder and louder until I could no longer ignore it. It about broke me, but deep down, I knew that this monumental "no" was about to set me up for a mighty "yes" in the future.

Time has shown me that the "no" and the "not now" are always for the best even when it doesn't feel that way. Even as I write this, I have no earthly idea what God is plotting on during this season of my life, but I am committed to obedience. Even in my darkest moments, my mantra has simply been, "Lord, I trust you." Thus, I'm reminded to be still and let Him work His magic. Patience is all about mindset. We have to stop worrying so much about what we want and when we want it and realize that while we feel like we are treading water in the moment, God sees our lives from a standpoint of forever. What you are hoping and fighting for may actually be selling yourself short. Be patient. Embrace "the wait" with anticipation and gratitude. Use the "wait time" to develop yourself and be ready for whenever the "not now" becomes a "yes!"

Questions for Consideration

1. When was the last time you rushed something that you wished you had practiced patience for?
2. Why do you think it's so hard for us to be patient for the things we want in life?
3. Create a short mantra for yourself that you can recite when you need to remind yourself to be patient. Write it down and place it somewhere visible.

Jewel Challenge

Remember that there is a distinct season for everything in life. Timing truly matters and can mean the difference between trying to fit a square into a circle and your happily ever after. Remind yourself that while ambition and running to-do lists are key to success, so are discernment and patience. Sit still and focus inward because the universe is always devising a plan in your favor. Your time is coming!

The Wait

In 2020, God put us all in TIME OUT! That's what my gut told me about the quarantine. So many of us were gearing up for the craziness that the month of March was going to bring, and it all came to a screeching halt. Instead, many of us experienced some much-needed time with our families and the opportunity to refocus on what truly matters. I don't know about you, but there's some things from quarantine that I want to move forward in my "new normal." Plain and simple, I want more time at home, and I want to continue being obedient to my purpose.

While I greatly enjoyed the "break," I often couldn't stop thinking about all of the plans I'd made that were now cancelled, postponed or forever changed. 2020 was about to kick off with a bang and for a while, it was literally driving me crazy not to fulfill the plans made. But... Some of the greatest things in life we must wait for. No matter how bad we want them, no matter how right now seems like the right time in our eyes; sometimes the only thing we can do is sit still and wait our turn.

The hardest thing in the world to do is to be full of passion and desire for something and have to wait to pursue it. A farmer cannot harvest great crops overnight. She/he must plant seeds, fertilize them, nurture them, and protect them. It takes time, so we cannot expect all things to come to fruition immediately or when we think it should. Patience and persistence truly are key.

Be truly present in what's in your presence. Understand that you are where you are for a reason, maybe even for a specific lesson. Embrace this part of your journey, it will ensure that you are ready to receive the ultimate prize!

Questions for Consideration

1. What is something you are waiting for? What additional lessons do you think you may need to learn before receiving your prize?
2. We live in a society that wants everything right now. What are some ways to stay grounded during "the wait?"
3. Who can you enlist to remind you to slow down and not settle when you get anxious and impatient?

Jewel Challenge

Practice your persistence! Remember that the universe is always working in your favor. All things happen in perfect timing. Work hard toward your goals. Do your part and trust that what's for you will come. Believe me, nothing worth having will require you to sacrifice your morals or values. The prize is worth the wait!

No Shame in a Setback

During the course of this book, we've talked about walking in your purpose and success. We've talked about fear but we have not talked much about failure. In the pursuit of anything great, most likely you will take missteps. You may fall flat on your face. You may be greatly ashamed and embarrassed, but what matters is what you learn during the process. I believe that we grow more from failures than we do from successes. Through failure our character is tested, we learn valuable lessons, and we are humbled.

"An inevitable part of discovering what we're good at is discovering what we're not. Anyone you see out there putting their gifts and experiences to full use with profound effectiveness has had a lion's share of misses. They fell forward as often as they leapt forward." ~Beth Moore

I was sitting on an airplane coming home from my friend Brittney's wedding, reflecting deeply over the beauty of her husband Patrick's love for her and how that manifested during the ceremony. The genuineness of it stung my heart but opened my eyes to the fact that I had settled. I was engaged to be married, yet on this trip alone. In our home, I was alone and isolated, fearful to be my true self for fear of criticism and rejection. I knew in my heart it was finished but I didn't want to admit it. For the sake of not having to end another engagement, I wanted to try my best to make it work. On that trip home, I knew I had nothing left to give. I couldn't make him love me more. I couldn't make him stay committed to me. I knew that if I had any chance of becoming the woman I'd hoped to become, I had to make a very hard decision. A decision that would ultimately be the most liberating one of my life to that point. It freed me from the fear of starting over and the fear of "what will people say." It freed me from the fear of the future and the fear of never finding my soulmate. Looking back now, I can tell you that for a while I was willing to manage disrespect, deceit, and infidelity because I was afraid to be alone. Today, I scream to you as loud as my lungs will carry, you will never arrive at your happily ever after in any aspect of life (career, relationship, etc.) if you're unwilling to accept failure, learn from it, and move forward.

It's easy to look at someone's success and think that it came easily; they make it look easy, don't they? It can be easy to assume that they have it made and that somehow, they had a greater plan for their lives than we had for our own. It's unfortunate, but even when the spotlight shines on folks the brightest, there's minimal illumination of their journey and the struggles that actually got them there. Don't allow a temporary failure or a setback to determine your future. Take the time to gather all the lessons you've learned on the journey and pivot toward your glory. Remember, it takes an infamous battle to create a legendary warrior! Just don't quit.

Questions for Consideration

1. What is it about our society that makes us afraid to fail? Why don't we share our stories of failure?
2. Instead of counting a failed situation as a waste of time or an embarrassment, how can you learn from the journey?
3. When was the last time you failed at something? What did you learn from the situation?

Jewel Challenge

Count your failures or setbacks as successes. Although they may be hard to swallow at times, they are badges of honor indicating that you tried and survived. You are still standing! There is no shame in a setback. Your time is coming. Stay focused, stay committed, and keep pushing!

Are you willing to say, "I'm sorry?"

Best-selling author, international speaker and leadership coach, Justin Patton, was a guest speaker in my nursing course one summer. A dear friend of mine, Justin, shared a story with the students about the importance of living your values. In his remarks about leadership, he noted that leaders are successful because their character always remains intact, not simply because of their intellect or expertise. He shared that once in an airport, he had an unpleasant interaction with a TSA agent that would have left her with an impression of him that was not a reflection of his values or the person he aimed to be every day. Instead of saying, "no big deal, I'll never see this lady again," he chose to go back and make the situation right (or at least offer an apology for his part in their exchange). Wow!

How many times do we get caught up in a situation, act in a way that is unbecoming, and go on as if it never happened? How often do we allow the conviction to make something right, pass us by because we don't want to acknowledge our part in the drama or misunderstanding? How many times have you said or done something that hurt someone and you never went back to address it? We often say things we don't mean when we are angry and when we act or react without thinking things through, we can end up hurting both strangers, and people who matter the most to us. We create scars that won't soon heal; scars that could forever damage a relationship that's extremely valuable to us; scars that cause trauma and impact the other relationships and interactions our loved one will have. No one really wants that!

We often get caught up being busy and neglect what really matters. We microwave from one life situation to the next without any resolution or healing. During my pageant training, my "mommy" Mrs. Denise, used to ask me what words best described me. She wanted to also know the words I wanted the judges to think of me as I competed. Some of the words I've used in the past were tenacious, compassionate, regal, and ambitious. As I thought through my performance in every area of competition, my goal was to leave the lasting impression of those three words on my audience. The same should be said in everyday life. Today, my words would include authentic, audacious, compassionate, convicted, attentive, and steadfast. My goal each day is that my behavior, both seen and unseen, is a reflection of my values. Don't leave the TSA Agent,the grocery store clerk, your partner, or your family member with a bad taste in his/her mouth. It's important to own up to your shortcomings. Brene Brown wrote: "I do want to live by my values and it's ok to be imperfect and make mistakes in this house. We just need to make it right when we can."

Perfection is never the goal. You may be royal but you are human. We all make mistakes. When you do, just make it right.

Questions for Consideration

1. What are your words? Take a moment to think about three words that you would like people to use to describe you.

2. Do all of your daily interactions with people reflect these words?

3. What about your social media posts? The way you deal with your family? Are you building a legacy that YOU would be proud of?

Jewel Challenge

Practice humility this week. Sit still and think about times you have said or done something that hurt someone you care about. If there's been no resolution between you and that person, contact them and apologize. Let them know that your behavior was not a reflection of your values and share your words with them. Be mindful of your words in every interaction no matter how big or small. Let those three words build the foundation of your legacy!

Control your Emotions

Emotion- a natural instinctive state of mind deriving from one's circumstances, mood or relationships with others.

Emotions are extremely powerful. They provide us with instincts that will tell us the best way to respond in any given situation but sometimes can get us into trouble. Sometimes we overreact and assume the worst, creating a meteor shower in our lives when all we needed to be prepared for was a light sprinkle. Acting solely out of emotion can cause irreparable damage in our lives.

Our emotions always have a history. Whether we want to admit them or not, they come from somewhere. I learned the hard way in my late 20's that I struggled with separation anxiety. I always needed to be sure that the people I loved and cared about were where they were supposed to be at all times. I learned that I loved folks intensely out of fear that they might leave, and I'd be left to do life alone...forever.

During the first session I'd ever had with a therapist, she asked me one question that turned a bright spotlight on where this came from. She asked me to take her back to when I was 13 years old and describe what I saw. Immediately, tears rushed to my eyes. There was so much repressed pain, fear, and confusion sitting on my spirit that I hadn't realized. I'd been carrying all this baggage around for years, functioning and coping but never truly healing and it was taking a major toll on every relationship I had. When I added in life's normal disappointments, cheating partners, unexpected deaths, and the stress of my career; I really needed help working through these emotions in a healthy way. I knew that being emotionless was not the answer but I also knew that being hypersensitive wasn't going to bode well in life either. I needed to effectively control my emotions; we all do.

Emotions are fickle and ever changing. This is the reason why it is dangerous to do things based on high emotion without giving plenty of consideration to everything involved. It's easy and sometimes natural to react, but it's not always easy to clean up the mess you've made by overreacting. I know we live in a world overrun with reality TV drama and social media beefs but behind closed doors and sometimes publicly, those actions and reactions have consequences. How do you prevent yourself from creating a meteor shower out of a light sprinkle? Just take a moment to think it through.

Not every situation requires a response. Not every confrontation needs to be had and not everything you feel needs to be said (or posted on social media). We must be mature enough to discern when we need to react/respond and when we don't. If your personal boundaries are being disrespected or you're in danger, by all means speak up! If you've somehow become the topic of gossip or "hating," let it go. The way you lead your life and the success you have in store will outweigh anything you'd have to say in the moment. Uncontrollable emotional outbursts are not effective. Just because it's the "norm" doesn't make it normal. Don't let the low standards of others downgrade your life. Control your emotions so they don't control you.

Questions for Consideration

1. Why do you think it's the norm for us to react first and ask for forgiveness later?
2. Think of a time when you've overreacted in a situation. What happened? How would you handle the situation differently if the same scenario presented itself today?
3. There is a major difference between controlling your emotions and being emotionless. How would you explain the difference?

Jewel Challenge

Take control of your emotions. Invest some time and energy into figuring out what your triggers are and where they come from. Stop letting what you did/didn't have in the past sabotage the possibilities of your future. When you feel yourself getting worked up, try to take a moment — don't react right away. Find a healthy outlet and if you need to address it, do so once you've calmed down. Being royal requires having restraint.

Sparkle Face

My pageant coach and mommy, Miss Denise, told me that "sparkle face" always wins and boy, was she right! "Sparkle face" is essentially the name she gave to the girl who lit up the stage. This girl sparkled the whole competition, appeared to have a genuine smile and looked like she was having the time of her life up there. The judges always looked forward to seeing her on stage in each phase of competition. She connected with them and compelled them to watch her every move. Sparkle face isn't necessarily something she could teach me. Essentially, it's a state of being that exists when you know you've done your best to prepare and you're ready to let the chips fall where they may. Sparkle face exudes confidence; it says this is me, take it or leave it. It says, I've already won regardless of whether or not you choose to crown me as YOUR winner today.

I bring up "sparkle face" because it can and should exist outside the pageant world and should be present in your everyday life. It's easy to get down in the dumps with all of the negative things happening around you but that's not your job. Your job here on earth is to shed light and to bring happiness to those around you. Be the light. We desperately need that positive energy in the world today. Not only will "Sparkle Face" change the people around you, it will change you. It will lift your mood, improve your confidence, and increase your ability to connect with others.

My hairstylist has a sign up in her shop that says, "Don't let anyone dull your sparkle." I couldn't agree more. Shine on!

Questions for Consideration

1. Who is someone you know with a consistent "sparkle face?" What about them makes them sparkle?
2. Why can achieving "sparkle face" be difficult? Why might we dull our sparkle sometimes?
3. What would it take for you to exude that sparkle daily and be the light in the room for others?

Jewel Challenge

Put your "sparkle face" on! Be the person others can't wait to see walk into the room. Let light and energy exude from you no matter the situation. It will be contagious!

Check your Position

Are you in the right position to receive what you say you want?

My pastor and spiritual advisor, Dr. F. Bruce Williams once said, "Any place worth going to is worth preparing for." To me, this means it is not enough to simply speak things into our futures, we must prepare ourselves to receive them. Take a moment to really think about that. Oftentimes, when we are on the cusp of something great, we face significant adversity. I'm talking about the type of adversity that will make you look up to the heavens and yell out to God, "ENOUGH! I cannot take any more!

In one month's, time, I lost my father who was my life's biggest cheerleader; I said goodbye to a marriage I just knew would conquer the test of time and my business partner decided that she wanted out. In one month's time, God uprooted me from everything I thought I knew and asked me to trust Him. I found myself on my knees day in and out, drowning my pain with hymns and prayers telling God that I had no idea where he was taking me, but that I trusted Him. In my deepest pain, I was reminded of the phoenix. This beautiful and mystical creature is only able to rise after the fire. Sometimes our entire lives have to be set on fire in order to prepare and position you for the season of abundance to come.

I have learned that there is always a lesson in the struggle, and it's a lesson you must master before you are truly able to walk in your purpose and receive your blessing. This part is all about mindset. If our thoughts center on loss and lack, we will constantly dwell in that place. There are no opportunities for growth in this space. Who you are and where you are currently is the residual manifestation of your past thoughts and actions...your mindset.

In the book, *"Outliers,"* Malcolm Gladwell discusses the 10,000 hour rule noting that it takes 10,000 hours of deliberate practice to become a world class expert in any given field. To that end, just as it's impossible to be an attorney without completing law school, it's impossible to be a good husband, wife, parent, or partner without investing in your own physical and mental health. It is imperative to heal from past hurts and pains. If you aim to be the royalty you were born to be, you cannot be content with seeing the world through the lens of negativity.

Invest time and energy into yourself to ensure that you are properly positioned to receive what you aspire to have. Amazing things seldom happen by chance. People are successful in all aspects of life, including relationships, because they are prepared for the next opportunity that may present itself. Even though God knew that Esther was the chosen one, she still had to endure a season of preparation prior to meeting the king. Be prepared for your coronation!

Questions for Consideration

1. Are you living your life in a way that is conducive to securing the gift you say you want for your future?
2. Is your walk in alignment with your talk? Are you actively taking steps toward your goals?
3. What are your goals for personal growth in the next year? List at least 3.
4. List 3 professional goals you'd like to see manifest in the next year.

Jewel Challenge

Check your position. Make sure that you are putting the work into preparing yourself and your environment to lead the life you want to live. Look at your list of goals from questions #4 and ask yourself if you are truly ready to receive any of those blessings. If your answer is not an emphatic YES, revisit question #3 and get to work! Your future depends on it!

Fourth Quarter:

Your Royal Mindset

because your reign is only as good as your
mindset...

Fight the Fear

For a decade, I knew that I wanted to be my own boss. I dreamt of owning my own women's health practice but year after year I told myself it wasn't time. I thought I didn't have enough experience and I'd never be able to afford it. I had folks in my ear saying it was crazy to leave a steady paying job and guaranteed paycheck to go out on my own. Ultimately, I was afraid of failure and the risk I'd be taking. I knew I wasn't completely happy with my current employer but was it time?!

One day at work, I walked into an exam room to perform an annual exam. My patient was sitting there in her paper outfit sobbing. It was two hours past her scheduled appointment time, she had only taken the morning off at her job, and was worried she'd be fired. In that moment, I was done. This was NOT what I signed up for. I knew I needed to be in a space where management cared about people over numbers, where women's time was respected, and where they were never rushed through their visits for the sake of the daily quota. That day, I realized that I had been settling in my career. I had gotten comfortable. It was time to fight the fear.

Eight months later, Athena Health and Wellness opened its doors and while it was a dream come true, there was more fear. What if no one came? What if we failed? I only saw 5 patients in the first month. I was terrified! But, the numbers gradually increased. We stayed the course despite the fear and the critics who were sitting back hoping we'd fail. Today, we have a couple thousand women who rely on us for services. It is literally a dream come true!

There is a certain level of fear that comes with taking risks. I've felt it before every big moment in my life. However, there is a significant difference between the anxiety you feel while taking a step to change your life and being so fearful that you never allow yourself to grow beyond your current situation. Beyond this, we must stop living in the realm of "what if." In the Beth Moore study on the Biblical book of Esther, she says, "When you say 'What if' the IF is an acronym for "I Fear." She couldn't have been more right! Living a life full of "IF's" is synonymous to living a life disheveled by fear. Think about it!

Failure is not a final destination. It is a fixed moment in time related to a specific event or situation. It does not define you or your potential, it is not your destiny. In fact, failure is a notch in your belt or experience that you can learn from to aid in your future successes. Be willing to try something new for the sake of excellence. Trust the process and be willing to endure the fear to get what you say you want.

Fear truly is the thief of all dreams. Fear of failure causes you to never try. Fear of criticism causes you to silence your voice. Fear of loss causes you not to enjoy the gifts you've been blessed with. Fear of betrayal causes you to never experience the beauty of trusting another person. Fear of uncertainty causes you to never take a risk. Fear of change causes you never to grow or evolve. Fear of vulnerability causes you to live superficially, without any depth or real connection. Fear is an emotion. One of the strongest, oldest, and most hardwired manipulators of the mind. Choose to live in fear or choose peace. You cannot have both!

Questions for Consideration

1. In Sheryl Sandberg's book "Lean In," she poses a profound question that I want to pose to you. "What would you do if you weren't afraid?" Really think hard about that question and be honest with yourself. What would you pursue if you weren't afraid of failure? A new job? A degree? Love? Making amends with your family? Starting your own business? What is that one thing that twenty years from now you will regret never trying?

2. Create a plan with measurable actions and a timeline to pursue each goal.

3. Share your plan with an accountability partner.

Jewel Challenge

Protect your joy and protect your potential by policing your thoughts. Don't jeopardize your future by allowing "What If's" to keep you stagnant. Stay grounded in today. Plan for tomorrow by taking one step NOW. Do it afraid. Trust me, your future self will thank you!

Audacious Living

Do we truly pursue anything audaciously (with boldness and without being held back by fear)?

I start this jewel with this question because I've experienced fear of completely "selling out" in pursuit of a goal; mostly because of fear of failure. In my first year of competing for the title of Miss Kentucky, I placed 1st runner up or 2nd place. The next year, I knew in my heart that the crown would be placed on my head on final night. I spent the entire year focused solely on that goal. I fine-tuned every skill I had, increased the difficulty of my talent routine, got in better shape, and hit the stage that summer ready for my reign to begin! Low and behold, I didn't even get my name called into the Top 10! You can imagine how devastated I was. Was all of this hard work in vain? What happened?

After the final competition, while I was trying my best to maintain poise and composure, I was approached repeatedly by people telling me I should try again and asking if I'd come back for my last year. In my mind, I had already decided that I wouldn't compete again. I was done! That winter, the University of Louisville announced that they were bringing back the Miss U of L competition after 67 years, and as big of a U of L fan as I am, I couldn't resist entering. I signed up knowing that if I won, the road would lead back to the Miss Kentucky stage. I won Miss U of L and this time around, I still trained hard, but I wasn't totally into it as I had been before. I was scared to "fail" again. I was scared to say out loud that I was going to win or that I truly wanted to be Miss Kentucky. That year, I placed Top 10 and it is the only regret I have in my life to this point. I should have pursued that year audaciously. On the other side of competing,I realized that I didn't lose anything at all regardless of the outcome. I became a much better version of myself, a version that my childhood self who lived on 18th and Hill Street in the West End of Louisville would have never recognized.

We all have goals and dreams (owning a business, financial freedom, finding true love, etc.), but only some of us truly pursue them. Why? Often our pasts are so flanked with pain and disappointment that we have a hard time thinking that our future can be any different. We succumb to the "this is how it will always be" mindset or to donating a significant amount of lip service without action because we are fearful. You may also have someone or several people in your life pumping your ear full of doubt and speculation. Understand this, royalty: Fear and audacity cannot coexist. It's impossible. That is a fact. Do not allow your fear of failure or past disappointments to rob you of the joy and excitement you will feel if you just go for it! Remember that the only true failure in life is not trying.

Questions for Consideration

1. What are your biggest dreams/goals?
2. Are you pursuing them audaciously right now?
3. When you have a big goal or big idea, what stops you from pursuing it? How can you remind yourself every day to pursue your passions while overcoming fear?

Jewel Challenge

My challenge for you is simple, live in victory and not in regret. Allow yourself to pursue things in your life audaciously. When you notice negative thoughts creeping into your mind or have negative people giving you poor advice, recognize the fear and block it immediately. Control the narrative you are telling yourself. Do it scared! Your future truly depends on it!

Just Do It

Have you had a magnificent idea that you feel in your gut that if you execute it, it'll change your world? You're so certain that this idea will pan out and bring immense abundance to your life, but before you put it into action, you've forgotten the idea all together? Don't you just hate that? I keep an ongoing list of future businesses I'd like to pursue or own one day and I create action steps and timelines toward reaching each of them. Each idea starts with research. Some end up being dead ends, some are ready to be put in motion immediately, and others have to wait, but all of them get an immediate once over.

It's often said why put off until tomorrow what you can do today and I truly believe that. If 2020 and 2021 taught us nothing else, it taught us that tomorrow is never promised. We have to take action today. For example, finishing this book has been on my goals list since 2016 and it didn't happen until I created a timeline for myself and seriously got into the research for editing and publishing. I just had to do it. I carved out time in my daily routine each day to write, reread, edit and meditate over my writing to ensure it was something I could confidently put out into the world. I had to get intentional about making the goal a reality.

Beyond creating action steps toward the goal, we must be mindful of what I like to call "time stealers," those things we do everyday that zap time and energy without us even noticing. Social media and television immediately come to mind as top time stealers. For example, I hardly watch television at home and I have the "Do Not Disturb" feature on my phone set from 10pm – 7am to ensure I have time before bed and first thing in the morning to do some purpose work. I do not allow myself to get on social media for the first hour I am awake and for the last hour before bedtime. It's all about creating the mindset, intention and opportunity to achieve the desires of my heart.

We all have goals and they may seem too big to pursue right now so we mentally surrender to not taking action and saying that we will get to them in the future. But when is that? It rarely seems like "now" is a good time to work on those goals but you really should. Time waits for no one. Just do it!

Questions for Consideration

1. What is one goal you'd like to accomplish this year?
2. Create a timeline with action items and measurable steps toward achieving this goal.
3. List 3 time stealers that decrease your ability to be productive and work on your goals. Create a plan to work around these time stealers so that they are less of an issue.

Jewel Challenge

There's no time like the present and tomorrow is never promised. Develop a sense of urgency about reaching your goals. Ask yourself a year from now, what will you wish you had started working on today? Once you have your answer, get to work!

Free your Mind

My grandmother once made a statement about the importance of having a positive outlook on life. She said, "If you look for negative you will find it." This statement, however simple it may be, was so profound and has always stuck with me.

I don't know how many times I've scrolled on social media and seen posts like the following.- "Today is going to be a bad day, I can just feel it,." "I'm not in the mood today so just leave me alone." "My job sucks." "I hate it when…"

Now, people are surely entitled to think and post what they want but my question is, why create a negative prophecy for yourself? Thoughts and words expressed into the universe become things in our lives. Why continue to exude more negativity into the world? Each day we have a very clear choice to make. We can wake up and allow ourselves to stay on the wrong side of the bed. We can allow our minds to play the woe is me card and succumb to walking around with a sour face and a bad attitude, surely adding to any problem around us. On the other hand, we can take control of our thoughts and see the blessings in every breath we breathe. We can choose to look for a way to make a difference and spread kindness and love all around us. It's very simple, and very easy to commit to IF you really want to.

There is no person or daily commitment on this earth that has the power to make or break your day without your consent. Yes, bad things happen. Yes, people come to you with drama and negativity. Yes, people can be unkind, they lie, they cheat, they steal, they gossip, but they cannot change your mood or impact your ability to be successful, if you don't let them.

Look for positive things in life and you will find them. Think about achieving and you will achieve. I find that while this appears to be a very simple concept, it can be hard to do. The world is negative and the media thrives off drama, sadness, and suffering. The law of attraction is simple. Whatever thoughts you are allowing to dominate your mind, you are attracting into your life. If you think about being miserable and negative, nothing will change. You will live constantly in that space.

Over the last year, I have implemented a daily meditation practice into my life.When I wake up in the morning, before my feet hit the floor, I grab my cedarwood essential oil and my phone. I'll scroll through the Breethe app and find a short meditation that addresses whatever I'm feeling in that moment. I'm intentional about my mindset because I know how much it impacts outcomes of the day and I truly can't afford any negativity. This meditation along with the rest of my morning routine is hands down the most important 30 minutes of my day.

Instead of saying I can't or this won't happen or I will never be good enough, start saying I will, I hope, I'm working toward something great and I am worthy of said achievement. Understand that where you are right now is a physical manifestation of the thoughts that go on in your head. Choose your thoughts wisely. They will make or break you!

Questions for Consideration

1. Why is it so easy for us to dwell in a mental space of negativity?
2. Create a mantra for yourself that you can recite when you find yourself overrun by negative thoughts or when there's something unsightly going on in the world around you.
3. Who can you charge with being your accountability partner? Identify one or more people and assign them their task.

Jewel Challenge

Check your mentality. Stop putting negativity into the universe, there's already enough there. When you feel negative thoughts creeping into your head, replace them with positive ones. Remind your friends or partner to call you out when you're getting sucked down the rabbit hole of negative thinking. Remember this...You are in charge of your mind. Your mind is not in charge of you.

Stop and Think

Over the last several years, I have transitioned to a more natural lifestyle. I made the decision to get rid of all of the chemicals and processed products I had been using and replaced them with essential oils, natural deodorants, and body products. The more I've paid attention to what's in a lot of the products I was using, the more I can't believe I'd ever used them. During this process, I started asking myself, "Why do we do so many things that are harmful to us?" Beyond the things we put on our bodies every day, I started thinking about other things like smoking, excessive drinking, engaging in toxic relationships, and putting ourselves in compromising situations. Why do we do things that we know will ultimately harm us?

My only answer is that it's customary. We were brought up this way and repeat what we saw in our families. The way our culture is set up, we do harmful things every day and perceive them as normal. We get comfortable in our daily habits. We negatively impact our own lives, complain about the way things are but don't take the time to assess why we are in the situation and how we can (sometimes easily) get out of it. Ask yourself this- Are you one of the people who address the symptoms of stress and anxiety or one who will change the behaviors that are causing it? Change is hard. If we stop and think about it, we can acknowledge that many things we do daily aren't good for us.

I'm not suggesting it's easy to change everything overnight. It took me over a year to completely transition my home into a toxin-free living space. My goal was 1-2 product replacements per month. For example, in month 1 laundry detergent and dryer sheets were switched to a plant based alternative and wool balls. The next month was soap, then dish detergent, deodorant, etc. It took time, but I did it! Especially now with toddlers on the loose, I have so much peace knowing there's nothing under the cabinets that can harm them, it's all natural!

Our personal lives are no different. We start by creating boundaries that best protect our values and then enforce them one by one in our relationships. Eventually, people come to realize that you mean business and certain things they cannot get away with when dealing with you. Every now and then, you may catch yourself in an old habit, but that's when you stop and think,- "Why am I doing this?"

Remember that life has no restart feature, rewind, or undo feature. You cannot take anything back. No matter how big or small, everything we say and do has consequences. Stop and think!

Questions to Consider

1. Think through a day in your life. What is something you routinely do that you have no real reason for?
2. What's something that is currently causing negative effects in your life or has potential to

cause negative effects that you would like to change?

3. Create a plan to change a negative to a positive. Share it with someone you trust to hold you accountable.

Jewel Challenge

Stop unnecessary and unhelpful habits.. Start thinking about all of the things you are putting on your body, in your body, and in your life and analyze them thoroughly. Are they good for you? If your answer is no, make a change. Your body, your future, and your peace of mind will thank you later!

Be Present

We live in a society powered by convenience and access. Our entire worlds are programmed into our cell phones and when you throw in social media and text messaging, it's a wonder we ever pay attention to anything in front of us. One evening, I was out to dinner with a friend after a typical busy day. As we sat down, their phone rang — a business call, not out of the norm at all for them, and then my phone vibrated. First, there was a text about something going on at Athena, followed by a text that Miss Kentucky needed something that would require a quick email and then there was a text from one of my girlfriends. The next thing I knew, the waitress had walked up to take our order. I ordered my meal, hardly looking up from my phone, then my friend ordered. What I hadn't realized is that she had been off the phone for a couple of minutes and had just been sitting observing me reentering my rabbit hole of unending work.

When I looked up, we shared a laugh, but then I immediately thought about how much time we spend with our heads down, checking email, texting, and scheduling the next aspect of our lives while missing what's right in front of us. I looked around the restaurant and everyone was essentially doing the same thing. There were couples at dinner, both distracted by their phones, kids trying to get their parents' attention from their phones, and kids playing on their parent's phones. We were all distracted!

It is OK to be busy, OK to live a boss life, OK to plan, and OK to position yourself to have multiple streams of income. My bestie, Mo and I are severe Type A personalities. We both find ourselves going from one goal to the next checking the boxes of success, but never actually stopping to sit in the victory. We are always moving on to the next goal. This is something we have been trying to hold ourselves accountable to of late.

While it's amazing to dream about the future, you will never have peace if you cannot shut your brain off long enough to experience your NOW. Don't reduce the present to a means to an end. You may have a ton on your plate or there may be a storm going on back at the office or you may not be where you want to be in life right this moment, but this moment may possess something you need to take your next step. Don't miss it!

Recently, I read *The Power of Now* by Eckhart Tolle and this passage really spoke to me:

> *"Not to be able to stop thinking is a dreadful affliction, but we don't realize this because almost everybody is suffering from it, so it's considered normal...Thinking has become a disease. Disease happens when things get out of balance."*

Live in the moment. Yesterday cannot be altered, tomorrow isn't promised. All you ever have is right now. Being mentally present releases the burdens of the past as well as the worries of the future. Celebrate the beauty of today. Learn the lessons of today. Be present today.

Questions for Consideration

1. Being fully present means having your focus, attention, thoughts, and feelings focused solely on the task at hand. Think about your last 24 hours. Have you been truly focused on every human interaction, conversation, and experience you've had?
2. How can you "turn your brain off" long enough to enjoy time for self, family, and the things you love? What types of parameters do you need to set, in order to make sure the things that matter most to you get your full and undivided attention?
3. Who will you enlist to hold you accountable to being fully present?

Jewel Challenge

Schedule some time away from your phone, work, technology each day. Be present in each moment and truly experience it — each breath, vision, interaction, sound and smell. Those things will never return and will soon be nothing more than a memory. Be present to experience the beauty in your life. Be present to experience peace and true joy. You can do it!

Ambition

The greatest compliment my grandmother has ever given me was when she said, "You've never let anything or anyone stop you from chasing your dreams. "The first time she said this to me after I finished my Master's degree, I had to stop and think about what she truly meant. We are all faced with adversity in life including situations that threaten to throw us off course with our goals. We can either choose to be deterred or we can choose to push through. I have refused to allow the first to be an option for me. In my mind, success was the only way. I had to see the goals through. Quitting meant a return to the life of poverty I desperately hoped to escape or showing my younger brother that it was OK to give up when the going was tough. Neither of those were negotiable for me. The "why" for the pursuit of my goals was bigger than the "right now."

February 27th, 2021- 3 days before the start of Diamond Club, the Premiere competition for the doTerra US and Canada market, I found myself in a puddle of tears on my bathroom floor ready to throw in the towel before it ever got started. That afternoon, I'd stood alongside my father's casket, speaking on behalf of the family, and I came "home" to a new house with my boys in a move that would start the process of a divorce that shattered the world as I knew it. It was a heart wrenching day to say the least, and I had no idea how I could lead this team of dynamic women on this journey. I didn't think I had it in me, and I didn't want to do anything but wallow and figure out how to heal. Two of my leaders, Necolle and Tamecka snatched me up and reminded me of my why...the boys who needed to witness mommy rise like the phoenix after getting knocked off her axis. I planned to make sure that they were set up for a life doing what they desired and felt purpose driven toward instead of having to "do what they had to do" for the sake of making ends meet. I planned to set them up for greatness and this could be my first big step in that direction. They poured prayers and love into me and ensured me that I could do this and that it was a divine distraction to keep me focused on the goal. And we did it, we completed Diamond Club in 16th place in the US and Canada which won us the 3rd place prize package. I regrouped, stuck to the plan and we did it!

The word ambition implies that there is more than a dream. Anyone can dream or have a goal. Ambition implies a commitment to hard work to achieve that goal. I'm sure you've heard the saying that ambition beats genius 100% of the time. It's true. Anyone can have an idea and can talk about what they hope to achieve in the future, but only a few people will put that idea into action.

Anything worth having is worth busting your butt for. Whether it's your career or a happy marriage, starting a new business, or getting into shape, there will be obstacles to overcome. What determines whether or not you achieve your goal is not the level of difficulty of the obstacle you meet on the way, it's your ambition and tenacity in the pursuit of the goal.

Even when it's easiest and most attractive to let go, hang on. The most monumental change in your life could be on the other side of that decision.

Questions for Consideration

1. In your opinion, what are the top 3 things that deter people from following their goals?
2. What ideas do you have that you have talked about but not yet put into action?
3. What about being ambitious ensures success?

Jewel Challenge

Do not allow a temporary circumstance or situation to halt the vision you have for your future. People will think you're crazy and you're going to feel down and want to quit, but it's OK! Pursue the dream anyhow.

Control

Confession: I've lived much of my life as a control freak. My ambition, drive, competitiveness, and impatience often get the best of me. I live by a never-ending checklist and always have a plan in place for the next goal. Becoming a mother has taught me flexibility. Just when I think I have a perfect plan in place, something changes, and I have to adjust. I had to learn to be OK with that. I took the Gallop strengths finder test and Adaptability was my #34, dead last on my list of strengths. It's my weakest link. Although I have gotten better, when plans change, it can be hard for me, especially if it is last minute.

In some way we all want to be in control of things. We want to control our careers, keep our loved ones (family members/children, etc.) on solid paths, or plan step by step of our lives. While some control and purposeful guiding of your steps is important, the desire to control everything can be very unhealthy. It is unhealthy in relationships and it is extremely unhealthy in the workplace.

Understand that you cannot control people nor can you control the universe. The perception of control is truly nothing more than an illusion. No matter what you do or how much you stress yourself out trying to make or prevent someone from doing said thing, they will do what they're going to do. You cannot make an addict stop using drugs. You cannot make a cheater stop cheating. You cannot make someone love you. You cannot make your child become who you want them to become.. Let go! Instead of trying to control others and situations, control the one thing you truly have control over — you! Invest in yourself to ensure you are happy and at peace no matter what. Are you currently or are you becoming someone your peers can respect? Are you now or are you becoming someone you'd want to date or marry? Are you now or are you becoming someone your children will grow up and want to emulate? Are you putting in the work to reach that next goal or are you just talking about it and hoping for the best? Think about it.

It's truly exhausting to try to control your entire world. Focus on what you can and let the rest go. Most control issues stem from the fear of what if. Fear feeds off the narratives of "what if." Change the narrative in your mind and you'll change the trajectory of your life.

Questions for Consideration

1. What are you trying to control right now that you need to let go of?
2. When you get worked up about a plan gone sideways, how can you remind yourself to stay grounded in the things you can control?
3. Create a mantra to remind yourself to pivot when things go differently than you wanted them to.

Jewel Challenge

Accept that you cannot control everything or anyone. Know that even when you see folks about to run smack into a brick wall, you can't always stop them. People have to live and learn on their own and you cannot let them drive you crazy in the process. This week I want you to focus on releasing some of the reigns you are holding onto in your life and other people's lives. Watch how much more at peace you become. Choose freedom and peace over control and rigidity. Let go!

Insecurity

I had a "friend" once who always cracked jokes on the rest of our friend circle. . Though each of us women on the move took time out of our schedules to support her, she rarely, if ever, showed up for any of us. When she did, she turned someone else's moment into her own. It got to a point where the drama she brought into the group and the emotional lability she became on everyone else made it no longer a friendship worth saving. At that time, she made the breakup someone else's fault. She posted things on social media alluding to her followers that we were the issue and that we had wronged her or "moved funny" to explain her distance. It took restraint to keep it classy and trust that her narcissism and backstabbing behaviors would be revealed in due time. Have you ever known someone like this?

The definition of insecurity is uncertainty or anxiety about oneself; lack of confidence, self- doubt. Being insecure is just plain unattractive. We all have levels of insecurity and jealousy that rears its ugly heads sometimes but we cannot allow it to interfere with our relationships. Are you able to support someone else who is being successful in their career and personal endeavors even when you have not yet made it? Are you able to be in the background of someone else's special moment without inserting yourself into the spotlight? Are you clapping while others win? Don't just reply to these questions with your gut answers; truly think about the last time you were in that situation and how you behaved. When was the last time you offered a compliment to another person? Are you living "your best life" FOR social media? Are you comparing how many likes you receive to how many he/she gets?

Confidence is silent and insecurities are loud. Eleanor Roosevelt once said, "You wouldn't worry so much about what others think of you if you realized how seldom they do." Insecurities stem from fears of not being enough. Don't allow them to ruin your friendships, relationships, or families. Just because it's not your time to shine, doesn't mean your job is to sabotage someone else's happiness. Life gets messy because people take their own issues and insecurities and project them onto others. Don't be the person who makes others feel smaller after an interaction with you. Even when you feel unsure of yourself, make others walk taller around you. Remember, you will never fix yourself by breaking the spirit of others.

Questions for Consideration

1. What are three things you are insecure about?
2. How do these insecurities manifest in your life? What are ways they positively and negatively impact your life?
3. Where do these insecurities stem from? What have you experienced in life that has caused them?

Jewel Challenge

Check your insecurities. While insecure people can be quite entertaining, their unhappiness can be extremely dangerous. Forgive the past and forgive yourself of your flaws. Accept all of yourself every day as a work in progress. You are beautiful! You are strong! You are enough! Believe it!

Quit Comparing

I remember going through the Miss Kentucky contestant placement lottery when I was competing. During this process, contestants wait with bated breath to hear our names called. The sooner our name was called in the lottery process, the more options we had to choose our number for competition. This was a strategy because we didn't want to compete after a young lady with the same type of talent, who had a great swimsuit body, etc. We wanted to position ourselves in a place most optimal for making the judges remember us.

This particular year, my name was called early on. I had many placement options left, but I stood up and selected #1. The room came alive with whispers because people thought I was crazy! But at that moment, I was being completely honest with myself. I knew that if I sat back and watched the other girls compete before me, I would start comparing myself to them and lose my confidence and swagger. I would say well her body is like this and mine isn't, her talent is singing and mine is dance — will I have a chance? Instead of going through these motions and setting myself up for a mental freakout right before I competed, I chose #1...I decided that I'd set the tone and let everyone else be compared to the bar I set. It worked for me. That year, my first year competing, I placed 1st runner up to Miss Kentucky.

Many of us compare ourselves to other people to the point of detriment. Neither men nor women, are lacking images across media outlets telling us what we should look like and the way we should act in order to be "liked," appreciated or considered desirable. As a former model, I can tell you that the majority of the images we are using to determine our self-worth are not even real. By comparing, we lose confidence in ourselves, doubt ourselves, and settle on being less than we can be because we have our eyes on what we think other people have or are doing. Don't compare your life to a snapshot that displays a millisecond of someone's life. While the photograph is glorious, you have no idea what transpired before or after the camera was put down. Someone could be smiling on the outside and dying on the inside. Many folks are posting on social media to perpetuate a brand or establish an image when they are actually living an entirely different life. Don't get fooled or distracted. Remember, there's no one on this earth worth competing with and damaging your sense of self-worth.

I was once told that horses race with blinders on for a reason. They block out any other distractions and solely focus on their own race. Be that thoroughbred running in the Kentucky Derby. Watch your lane ONLY! Be the best version of you each and every day. Don't reduce your self-worth by comparing yourself to someone outside of your mirror. You are a masterpiece!

Questions for Consideration

1. In what ways do you feel incomplete, inadequate, or less than?
2. How do those feelings affect how you present yourself every day and how you interact with those around you?
3. If you truly put your blinders on to the outside noise and look into the mirror, what do you see? Remember, no comparing! Are you better than yesterday? Last week? Last year? If the answer is no, it's time to get to work on YOU and for YOU!

Jewel Challenge

My challenge for you is to be honest with yourself about your daily comparisons. Recalibrate your measuring stick. Maybe it's time to take a social media break or unfollow some people that trigger your insecurities. Be yourself. Compete only with yourself. Try to improve yourself every day, but also remember you were perfectly designed, flaws and all. Put your blinders on.

Vulnerability

There was a time in my life where I viewed vulnerability from a military sense and thought it meant to be weak and exposed to the possibility of being harmed or attacked. Essentially, living in a community that subscribed to the "what happens in this house stays in this house" mentality, I believed in keeping things in and only showing the world, including those close to me, what I wanted them to see. It took years for me to realize that there was another way. My late father, a frequent speaker at The Healing Place, told me one day after he spoke that I shouldn't be ashamed of my story. He told me that I should share it freely because you never know who it will help. At that moment, I realized something, I'd been living beneath my purpose. Why wasn't drug abuse prevention my platform when I compete in pageants? Why was I hiding my humble beginnings? I was trying to separate my history from my destiny and realized in that moment that there was another way. Brene Brown wrote, "Because true belonging only happens when we present our authentic, imperfect selves to the world, our sense of belonging can never be greater than our level of self-acceptance."

Vulnerability is not about being weak. It's about being authentic. It's saying you aren't perfect and neither is your past, but you can still be successful. You can still be great. Many of us are living bound to past mistakes and decisions, afraid that someone else will judge us for them when what we are truly doing is judging ourselves. When we present a façade to the world, what we are saying is I'm really not worthy and I'm not enough, so I'm hiding behind this likeable image of myself that I've created. It's one of the most subtle manifestations of insecurity.

> *"The truth is: Belonging starts with self-acceptance. Your level of belonging, in fact, can never be greater than your level of self-acceptance, because believing that you're enough is what gives you the courage to be authentic, vulnerable and imperfect."* ~Brene Brown

Vulnerability is about being real. It's what connects us to one another and it's what makes us human. None of us have it all together all the time. Literally, it's impossible. We need to stop hazing each other with these picture perfect ideals on social media and realize that it's ok to tell the truth about who we are and what we've overcome to get where we are today, even if we are not where we want to be. Your journey is a testimony. Encourage someone today and share your test!

Questions for Consideration

1. What keeps you from living a truly authentic life?
2. What story/test of yours should you be sharing that you've been afraid or unwilling to share?
3. How can you turn your test into a testimony? Create a plan to share your story in a way that can be therapeutic to others.

Jewel Challenge

Sharing really is caring and healing from our past does not begin until we are able to be honest with ourselves about where we've been and how it's shaped us. What is your real story? Have you healed from the traumas in your past? Have you used those scars to help others heal or prevent the same pitfalls all together? Your willingness to be honest and vulnerable could pull someone else out of a very dark place. Tell your story!

Crown Yourself

In today's world, we measure ourselves so often by the validation we receive from others. Our importance or significance is measured by the number of followers we have or the amount of "likes" we receive on social media. Many of us have become so obsessed with the perfect selfie or photo that we forget to live in the moment and truly experience things. Let me tell you that even the most perfectly filtered photo with thousands of likes does not translate to self-confidence, security, happiness.

This mindset creates an affinity for "perfection;" a goal or horizon one can never reach. Something that exists nowhere except in the mind. It's the reason why we compare ourselves and our lives to others. It's the reason we lie in relationships with people we care about and want to care about us. It's the reason we spend so much time crafting the perfect post for our followers on social media. It's one of the reasons why many of us are unhappy and are living within the grips of depression and anxiety. We're constantly wanting, lacking, and dissatisfied because what we aspire is simply unreal.

Your personality, your intellect, and your character are statements of where you have been in life thus far, but they are not statements of your potential or worth as an individual. Your past is not your final destination. Once we accept that we are good enough, smart enough, beautiful enough, qualified enough, etc., we are able to walk in our purpose daily and have peace of mind. In the words of my pastor, Dr. F. Bruce Williams, "You cannot live in peace with other people if you are not at peace with yourself."

It's time to start embracing our true selves completely. It's time to be vulnerable. You deserve to live in your truth every day and for those around you to know the real you. Contrary to popular belief, vulnerability does not represent weakness. The ability to be vulnerable demonstrates your strength, resilience, and ability to acknowledge that while you may be imperfect and a work in progress, you are still enough. Vulnerability allows you to be honest enough to set and uphold the standards of your life. It allows you to secure the life you desire and deserve. In the words of Brene Brown, "Vulnerability is the birthplace of love, belonging, joy, courage, empathy, and creativity. It is the source of hope, empathy, accountability, and authenticity. If we want greater clarity in our purpose or deeper and more meaningful lives, vulnerability is the path."

Questions for Consideration

1. Why do you think we are so inclined to care what others think about us?
2. What does the word vulnerability mean to you? Are you vulnerable with the people in your circle? If your answer is no, why?
3. It's been said that you cannot separate your past from your future. What about your past?

How can you use it as motivation or a testimony to build your future plans upon?

Jewel Challenge

Implement a mindset of growth. Don't try to be perfect. Work on improving your imperfections instead of trying to hide them. Our beauty marks, quirks, and annoying nuances are what make us unique; they are what make us beautiful. Remember, you are enough! You are amazing! You are royalty! Don't wait on the world to determine your value...Crown yourself!

Letter from the Author...to my sisters

Thank you for reading this book. It's been a labor of love and healing for me to write but I pray that it pours into your life in just the right way. I pray that you find jewels that will help you to take your life to the next level and pursue all that you deserve. I chose to end this book with one of my favorite blog pieces just as a reminder for each of my sisters specifically, and myself, that we truly are royal and worthy of the best. Come back to it any time you're doubting yourself or have forgotten who you are.

Dear Sis,

Sis, you are enough. The very essence of who you are at this moment should be celebrated. I know you have goals and dreams. You are imperfect yet amazing in the space you are in today. Celebrate exactly where you are in this moment while knowing that even though you may not be where you want to be, you are not where you used to be.

Sis, speak up! Use your voice. God gave you a perspective that only you have. You were made with a purpose to impact the world in a way that only you can. Do that. Be bold and stand proudly in the spaces that you occupy. Celebrate yourself by using your voice.

Sis, create and protect boundaries for yourself. You deserve to feel safe, have peace, be respected, and feel loved. Those things are the bare minimum required of people who want to share your space. Celebrate yourself by holding them firm.

Sis, trust your gut. We all have that spirit of discernment that tells us when to move or be still, speak or restrain, pursue or pass, and engage or disengage. That voice will never steer you wrong. Celebrate yourself by trusting the spirit to guide you in every way.

Sis, relinquish the illusion of control. Realize there's very little in this life that you actually have control over and stop spending time and energy worrying and stressing about things you can do nothing about. Celebrate yourself by letting everything else be as it may.

Sis, It's OK to take your cape off sometimes. Take time for yourself and turn off your phone or sit in your closet. Take a moment of silence or relax in that space and "let your hair down." There is nothing selfish about prioritizing yourself. Celebrate yourself by consistently practicing self-care.

Sis, there are no mistakes. God took his time on you. You are beautiful. You have a greater purpose than you could ever imagine. You were birthed from the

divine and are an heiress to the kingdom. Stand up straight and fix your crown. You are royalty and please don't ever forget it.

I Love You,

Made in the USA
Columbia, SC
21 February 2022

56171764R00065